YOUTH BIBLE STUDY GUIDE

Image & Self-Esteem

Youth Bible Study Guides

Sexuality

Following God

Image & Self-Esteem

Peer Pressure

Coming Soon . . .

God

Jesus Christ & the Holy Spirit

Sin, Forgiveness & Eternal Life

Church, Prayer and Worship

YOUTH BIBLE STUDY GUIDE

Image & Self-Esteem

COMPILED AND WRITTEN BY
CHIP AND HELEN KENDALL

Authentic

MILTON KEYNES ● COLORADO SPRINGS ● HYDERABAD

Copyright © 2009 Chip and Helen Kendall

15 14 13 12 11 10 09   7 6 5 4 3 2 1

First published 2009 by Authentic Media
9 Holdom Avenue, Bletchley, Milton Keynes, Bucks, MK1 1QR, UK
1820 Jet Stream Drive, Colorado Springs, CO 80921, USA
Medchal Road, Jeedimetla Village, Secunderabad 500 055, A.P., India
www.authenticmedia.co.uk

*Authentic Media is a division of IBS-STL U.K., limited by guarantee, with its
Registered Office at Kingstown Broadway, Carlisle, Cumbria, CA3 0HA.
Registered in England & Wales No. 1216232. Registered charity 270162*

British Library Cataloguing in Publication Data
A catalogue record for this book is available from the British Library

ISBN-13: 978-1-86024-630-2

Scriptures quoted from The Youth Bible, New Century Version (Anglicised Edition) copyright © 1993,
2000, 2007 by Authentic Media, 9 Holdom Avenue, Bletchley, Milton Keynes, MK1 1QR.

Extracts taken from:
Andy Flannagan, *God 360°*, Spring Harvest & Authentic, 2006
Maxine Vorster, *Hidden Hunger*, Authentic, 2006
Josh McDowell, *Youth Devotions 2*, Tyndale House, 2003
Ems Hancock and Ian Henderson, *Sorted?*, Authentic, 2004
Andy Frost and Jo Wells, *Freestyle*, Authentic, 2005
Chip Kendall, *The Mind of Chip K: Enter at Your Own Risk*, Authentic, 2005
Shell Perris, *Something to Shout About*, Authentic, 2006

'Be' Erick Cole, Kevin Max
© 2001 Blind Thief Publishing/Sad Astronaught Music/Up in the Mix Music/
Adm. by Small Stone Media BV, The Netherlands. Used by permission

Cover and page design by Temple Design
Print Management by Adare
Printed in Great Britain by Bell and Bain, Glasgow

If anyone belongs to Christ, there begins a new creation.
The old things have gone: everything is made new!

(2 Corinthians 5:17)

Chip and Helen spend most of their time on the road with thebandwithnoname, Innervation Trust's longest running touring band. As a band they've seen thousands of young people respond to their dynamic gospel presentation, and this is by far the most rewarding part of the job!

Chip's first book, *The Mind of chipK: Enter at Your Own Risk* has helped loads of young people grow in their faith. He also presents a weekly radio show (theshowwithnoname) on Cross Rhythms, with syndication across the UK. In addition, he absolutely loves his role as one of the key youth presenters for GOD TV. All of these jobs continue to pave the way for him to speak at events everywhere.

Helen loves dancing for thebandwithnoname, and gets to use her management skills as team leader for the band. She is also Assistant Director of Innervation, a ministry setting up loads of bands all over the UK. In addition she enjoys teaching for Genetik, a creative evangelism academy, and contributing 'Life Articles' for the Cross Rhythms website.

Chip and Helen currently reside in Stockport, England and they still have trouble understanding each other's accents.

Thank Yous

First up, thanks to Malcolm Down and the rest of the guys at Authentic for giving us the opportunity to work on these study guides, it's been a blast. To everyone at SFC who read the books and gave us your thoughts, we appreciate the feedback. Thanks to lovely Lucy West for the fantastic photos, and Kylie for the typing. To everyone who talked to Chip for the 'people clips', thanks for your honesty and willingness to put up with the quirky questions. A really huge thank you to Brian and Norma Wilson for their 'hidden pearls' of wisdom. We loved your perspective on things. Finally, big thanks to all the authors whose work we have used in this book. You are an inspiration.

CONTENTS

INSTRUCTIONS

The book you're holding in your hands is a study guide. It's a compilation of lots of other books written about this subject. It might not make you the world's expert on the subject, but it should give you lots of useful information and, even better, it should give you some idea of what the Bible has to say about . . . IMAGE & SELF-ESTEEM.

What is a 'reaction box'?

Throughout the book, you'll find these helpful little reaction boxes. We've added them so that you can decide for yourself what you think about what you've just read. Here's what one should look like once you've filled it in:

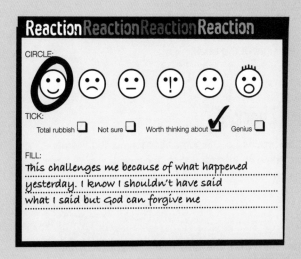

Pretty simple really . . .

Circle the face that reflects how you feel about it.

Tick the box that shows what you think about it.

Fill in any thoughts you have about what you've learned on the lines provided.

What are 'people clips'?

Just so you don't get too bored, we've added a bunch of 'people clips' to each study guide. These are people just like you, who were happy for us to pick their brains about various related topics. Who knows? Maybe you'll find someone you recognise.

What are 'hidden pearls'?

Everyone needs some good old-fashioned 'grandparently' advice, so we collected some pearls of wisdom from our friends Brian and Norma Wilson (aged 86 and 85), which you can find scattered throughout the book.

What is a 'reality check'?

Finally, throughout the book you will come across sections called 'Reality check'. These should provide a chance for you to apply what you've been learning to your own life experiences.

Other than that, the only rule that applies when reading this book is that you HAVE FUN!! So start reading.

Chip & Helen

INTRODUCTION

Basic needs

A few weeks ago, we heard someone say that the four basic needs of humans were acceptance, identity, security and purpose. We immediately tried to prove this assumption wrong and think of lots of things that didn't fit with those four but we couldn't. Take a minute to think about it: do you agree? The point is that it's not enough for us to have food, water, a house, some money (security) – that might be enough for animals but as humans we have many more needs. We need purpose, that means, a reason for living, something to work towards, a goal, things we look forward to. I think you'll agree that if you woke up every morning and you didn't have to do anything, you didn't have any plans for the future or even any plans for the next hour, life would get pretty depressing pretty fast (even though the idea of having no homework to do for a few days does sound appealing).

This book is going to focus on finding out more about the two basic human needs of acceptance and identity. We think they are linked. Often our identity is based on acceptance, we do certain things because we think that will make people like and accept us more – we dress a certain way, act a certain way, hang out with certain people, listen to certain music, choose a certain educational or career path and often it all has to do with getting people to accept us. Although we recognise that the need for acceptance is something that God put in us and therefore is a good thing, we want to challenge you to believe that your identity, who you are as a person, does not need to be based on what other people think. God has loads to say in the Bible about who you are and who he made you to be. He is such a creative God that he made us all different, we all have different irises and different fingerprints. Isn't that amazing? If he went to so much effort with eyes and fingers, we think he probably put the same amount of thought into every other part of you too.

A big part of growing up is figuring out who you are and who you want to become. Often we let other people, the media, our teachers, our friends shape who we become without giving it much thought. Hopefully, this book will help you to find out who God made you to be and to find your identity in him.

what does the Bible say about IMAGE & SELF-ESTEEM?

Body

Your Image

I praise you because you made me in an amazing and wonderful way. What you have done is wonderful. I know this very well.

(Psalm 139:14)

1

First up

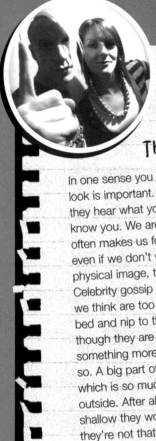

Ever heard the phrase, 'Image is everything'? Think it's true?

In one sense you can't get away from the fact that the way you look is important. It is the thing that people judge you on before they hear what you've got to say, see what you can do, or get to know you. We are visual creatures and the way people look often makes us form opinions and judgements in our heads even if we don't want to. As a society, we are obsessed with physical image, the way we look, the way other people look. Celebrity gossip magazines are filled with pictures of people who we think are too fat, too thin, or just had the cheek to get out of bed and nip to the shops without putting any make-up on, even though they are rich and famous! Imagine that! But is there something more to image than the way that you look? We think so. A big part of your image should be who you are inside, which is so much more important than how you look on the outside. After all, we've all met 'beautiful people' who are so shallow they would make a raindrop look deep, and in the end, they're not that much fun to be around.

In a culture that is saturated by media images and suggestions about how we should look, act, be, think, it is really hard to get and maintain a healthy, balanced sense of self-image. We hope this chapter will get you thinking about how important your image is to you, how you can get God's perspective on your image and how to survive in a world obsessed with looking young, thin and gorgeous.

Fashion factor

Gucci, Diesel, Adidas, Nike, Armani, Levi . . . we live in a world where everything has a label. Whether it's clothes, shoes, handbags, accessories or even socks, everything comes with a price – the better the label, the more expensive it is. But why? Why have clothes become such a huge part of our lives?

Fashion is such a pressure for young people, especially young girls. It's almost reached a stage where what you wear defines who you are. I would like to suggest something different to you . . . why don't you let God define who you are? You see, **GOD HAS CREATED EVERY BIT OF US,** our DNA, personality, character, brain, heart, soul, likes, dislikes, structure . . . everything. He knows exactly how many hairs we have on our head and loves us just the way we are. He doesn't care what clothes we wear or how fancy our hair looks, or how much our jeans have cost – he cares about our hearts and the way we are inside. If your heart is broken and your life is a mess, it's not going to go away by wearing expensive clothes. It's just going to cover it up.

I've been there myself. I went through a stage in my life where I wouldn't even answer the front door without any make-up on. Without even knowing, I was trying to cover up the pain in my life by wearing fancy clothes and wearing loads of make-up. It was kinda like a mask that I was wearing. Sure, it made me feel better about myself for a while but it didn't get rid of the fact that I was messed up inside. If only I'd have realised sooner that what I really needed was God . . .

God has created you and he loves you more than you could possibly imagine. He loves our good points and our bad points. He loves our hands, feet, head, knees, elbows, ears, eyes, heart . . . everything! People used to tease me so much about the way I looked and it used to really upset me but as soon as I started to realise that God loves me just the way I am, it totally changed me. Somebody once said to me, 'If you don't know how to love yourself, how can you love other people?' I still don't fully understand why God loves me but I know that he does and I'm learning more about God's love for me every single day. My advice to you is this . . . it's perfectly alright to wear nice clothes as long as that's not the most important thing in your life. Clothes may make you feel good about yourself but they don't last. You will outgrow them and they will get damaged but you will never outgrow God's love. Whether you are 3 or 93, God will keep on loving you and love you when you think he can't possibly love you any more – he will!

Shell Perris, *Something to Shout About*, Authentic, 2006

CIRCLE:

😊 🙁 😐 ⁉ 😕 😮

TICK:

Total rubbish ☐   Not sure ☐   Worth thinking about ☐   Genius ☐

FILL:

....

....

....

Hidden pearls

'I think it's good, as long as it's not indiscreet, that Christians should look smart – why shouldn't they? I remember when Billy Graham came to England for the first time, his wife had red fingernail polish on. Everyone was very shocked because Christians didn't have red fingernails at that time. But very quickly lots of young women also had red finger nails, and why not? There might have been red fingernails in the Bible for all we know.'

BODY IMAGE

The likelihood is that everyone has a part of their body that they are not keen on. It may be their freckles, muscles (or lack of them), the shape of their legs, their tummy, arms, hair, nails, teeth, nose – well the list is pretty endless. Even (and especially) supermodels who earn millions of pounds to look good are often so obsessed with what they look like that they channel huge amounts of their earnings into minor corrective surgery and beauty treatments. But guess what? There are only about fifteen supermodels in the whole world and yet people measure their own bodies against these people. How crazy is that?

 ur image of what is attractive has a lot to do with the mass media's idea of conventional good looks. These images lie to us that this is the only way to look attractive. They sell us dissatisfaction with who we are and what we look like. We also don't tend to see behind the smile to the facelift, Botox, skin tuck or crushingly low self-esteem.

The way that the world sees attractiveness is incredibly narrow, isn't it? What about people with larger noses, rounded tummies, crazy hair or big feet? Don't they have something to offer? Can they not look attractive? Of course they can and do.

The trouble with our society is that it bases how valuable we are on the way we look, rather than on the person we are. These days blokes get as hung up on their appearance as much as girls do. The pressure to look right is just as strong for them. In 1 Peter 3:4 it says: **'YOUR BEAUTY SHOULD COME FROM WITHIN YOU – THE BEAUTY OF A GENTLE AND QUIET SPIRIT THAT WILL NEVER BE DESTROYED AND IS VERY PRECIOUS TO GOD.'**

Sometimes we can look at ourselves as an object, because that is the way that the world causes us to think. We can treat ourselves like an item bought in a shop that is faulty and needs to be taken back or altered – something that wasn't perfect when it was created. We can easily allow an unhealthy view of ourselves to develop and take hold.

If you were asked to write three good things about yourself and three bad things, which would you find easier to do? Most of us are living from a script that someone else wrote for us. Think about some of the words that have been spoken over you: the curses such as fat, ugly, useless, stupid, insignificant, not as (whatever) as someone else. Maybe you have even said some of these things about yourself.

These are all lies that we can believe to be true. But this is not how God sees us or wants us to see ourselves. The voice and breath behind heaven says different. And he should know. He's the one that made you as you are.

As we have said, we are born to crave acceptance from others, and deep within us is the desire not just for others' approval but for God's!

There is no escaping our identity and God does not want us to. But there is no such thing as an ordinary or boring human being. **ALL OF US ARE GOD'S ADORED CHILDREN.** We are fought over, rescued people who have the most special place in the heart of God. He has chosen us, not left us by the wayside. He has picked us out, not kicked us out.

God does not see us as ugly, imperfect, spotty, greasy-haired monsters – even if that is what we feel like. He sees us with the same eyes of love that look at Jesus. He sees us with all the perfection, loveliness, beauty and joy of his Son. When we know Jesus, we start to become like him inside – as someone dearly loved and precious to God. The other stuff on the surface really doesn't matter to him, unless of course it stops us from being the people he has made us to be.

Remember what truly attractive people are? Interesting, fun to be with, kind, generous, trustworthy, enthusiastic, reliable, gentle, godly. None of these things depends on what we look like.

Ems Hancock and Ian Henderson, *Sorted?*, Authentic, 2004

Reaction Reaction Reaction Reaction

CIRCLE:

TICK:
Total rubbish ☐   Not sure ☐   Worth thinking about ☐   Genius ☐

FILL:

....

....

....

....

Name: **Sophie Lashford**

Age: **19 years old**

From: **The Midlands**

Current status: **Law student at Cambridge**

Craziest recent experience:

Living in a slum for 5 days at Soul Survivor!

Tell us about your experience of self-image:

'I've been living in China for the past year which has meant I've had a year where I can't read beauty magazines because I couldn't understand them. All the Chinese people I met always told me I was beautiful because they see foreigners as naturally beautiful. It's really built up my self-image but now suddenly I'm back in England and my friends are talking about weight all the time and here we're always not thin enough, not beautiful enough, or our nose is the wrong shape. God's really been challenging me not to fall back into thinking like that. It's not the way that God sees me: I'm beautiful and made in his image and he has so many more important things to tell me about.'

ARE YOU LOOKING TO THE MEDIA OR THE MASTER?

(Psalm 139:17)

One day Adam walks in from a hard day of tilling the soil. When he sees Eve, he drops his hoe in surprise. 'What's with the tiger fur? You always wear goat skins. I like you in goat skins.'

'Adam, darling,' Eve says with a little laugh, 'Goat skins are so out this year. Everyone's wearing tiger fur. Haven't you noticed on TV? Haven't you seen the fashion magazines? And by the way, I'd get rid of that cowhide outfit of yours if I were you. Sheepskin is all the rage with the guys these days.'

 – so maybe Adam and Eve figured out what to wear without the help of TV, magazines, movies and commercials. But nowadays it seems we can't get dressed without someone telling us what's hot and what's not.

The media screams that you have to look a certain way to be acceptable. Guys have to be tall, dark and handsome. Women beat themselves up if they don't have measurements in perfect proportion. If you want people to consider you good-looking, you'd better not have a bad complexion or wear the wrong clothes.

So the media has made up its own standard for what it considers to be a good-looking person. Maybe you believe that that standard is the ultimate standard. And if you don't look like that and live up to it, then you probably don't like the way you look.

Does that make it wrong to try and look the way the media says you should? Not usually – at least when it comes to clothes and other easy-to-swap styles. But if you're physically trying to match the media's ideal of a perfect body, look out, you are in for some frustration. Why? Two reasons. First, the media's standard is constantly changing. Don't whittle yourself down to 95 pounds if the media says skinny is in, because next year skinny will probably be out.

Second, you are constantly changing. Sure, you might look like a movie star today, but in a few years you will probably look more like how your father or mother looks today. That's just how it works. **IF YOU BASE YOUR SELF-WORTH ON THE WAY YOU LOOK, YOU ARE GOING TO BE FRUSTRATED.**

You need to base your self-worth on a value system better than the media's – God's. He was the master designer, chief architect and construction supervisor when you were put together in your mother's womb. He watched it all happen to make sure you came out just right. And he still thinks you're just right. Your basic design and appearance is his masterpiece.

REFLECT: HOW MUCH DO YOU TRY AND KEEP UP WITH TRENDS? WHEN DOES THAT GET IN THE WAY OF APPRECIATING THE WAY GOD MADE YOU?

PRAY: THANK GOD FOR MAKING YOU UNIQUELY YOU.

Josh McDowell, *Youth Devotions 2*, Tyndale House, 2003

ReactionReactionReactionReaction

CIRCLE:

😊 😦 😐 ⦵ 😕 😮

TICK:

Total rubbish ☐   Not sure ☐   Worth thinking about ☐   Genius ☐

FILL:

....
....
....
....
....

Make an effort

Helen talks

Over the years, I've played a game with lots of school kids where you have to dress up as various characters. We hand out a mixture of items ranging from funky disco wear to old grandad jumpers to sporty tracksuits. Each team has 1 minute to dress someone up as a particular character, such as a 'disco diva', 'sports freak' or 'Christian'. What we've found over the years is that over and over again kids in schools dress the Christian in the geekiest clothes they can find. They put on ugly brown trousers, big baggy old jumpers and 'Jesus sandals' without even giving it a second thought. Now I know it's just a silly game but it does get you thinking about how the world views Christians! It seems that lots of people think we look funny, are old fashioned and out of date.

Now I'm not about to say that all Christians should be dressed up to the nines all the time, at the height of fashion, of course not, but I am saying that we need to think about our appearance and how we represent Christ. While we are here on earth, we are the only representation of Jesus that most people will ever see (unless they have some amazing vision or something). **PEOPLE BASE THEIR OPINION OF GOD AND JESUS ON US, THE CHURCH, THE CHRISTIANS.** If we want to communicate to them that we serve a God who is relevant, has something to say to today's culture and is interesting, then perhaps we should start presenting ourselves well. I don't mean that we should all be the same and all dress in the current trends, but we should be the best at what we can be. We should make an effort with our appearance. Maybe your school makes you wear a uniform that you have no control over. Well, wear it well, make an effort. Do your hair, wash your face, make sure you put some deodorant on! Loads and loads of psychological studies have shown that people who look good get more opportunities in life, whether that's jobs, promotions, being picked for things. Of course I'm not saying that we should value looks above everything else, or that we should only be valued for the way we look, but we should make the best advantage of what we've been given. If you're going to a university interview or a driving test then iron that shirt, put on that tie, fix your hair . . . make an effort.

The same goes if you are hanging out with your friends, or going out to a party. In some ways, making an effort with the way you look shows respect to the people you are with, it shows that you are bothered enough to put some energy into getting ready to meet them. Obviously, all this needs to be done in a balanced way – I'm definitely not talking about tarting yourself up so that you can manipulate people or being shallow and only interested in looks.

1 Corinthians 6:19 says, '**YOU SHOULD KNOW THAT YOUR BODY IS A TEMPLE FOR THE HOLY SPIRIT WHO IS IN YOU.** You have received the Holy Spirit from God. So you do not belong to yourselves'. Sometimes as Christians we think God is only concerned with 'spiritual' things like how much we prayed, whether we read our Bible today, how many people we witnessed to. But this verse talks about our bodies, about the fact that the Holy Spirit lives in us. I think that means we should respect our bodies. If you knew that your favourite movie star or football player was coming to visit your room, you would make sure it was clean and tidy and looking good. It's the same with our bodies. If the Holy Spirit lives in us, we should think about what we put into our bodies, that includes food, drink, illegal substances, smoke. Are you treating your body well, as if it belongs to someone really important? Do you take care to eat things that will strengthen and nourish you or do you shove junk into your body all the time? Do you pollute your liver and kidneys with too much alcohol, or your lungs with cigarette smoke or are you careful to keep your body in as good a condition as possible. I reckon as Christians we should be setting examples in everything – that means we should be healthy, fit and well dressed. We should live in such a way as to show off Jesus, but with a humility that shows we are totally dependent on *him*.

Reaction Reaction Reaction Reaction

CIRCLE:

TICK:

Total rubbish ☐ Not sure ☐ Worth thinking about ☐ Genius ☐

FILL:

....

....

EXERCISING FAITH

Read 1 Timothy 4:1–8

I don't know if you're the sort of person who is meant to stretch every morning, for example to help your back, neck or shoulder. If you're like me, you often feel a bit guilty for not doing your stretches, and if you've also got guilt because you haven't spent time with God, then this exercise could be good for you. I'm walking very gingerly here (not because of a bad back), but because I don't want to fall into the territory of 'Praise Aerobics' videos!

It is actually quite a natural fit. Stretches work best when you take some time over them and do them very slowly. In fact they can be counter-productive if rushed. The same could be said of prayer. The concept is simple. While you're stretching, ask God to stretch you in the different areas of your life. Pray for the faith to occasionally sprint, taking risks and trusting his provision. Pray for the infilling of his Spirit to power your spiritual muscles. In the same way that an athlete's muscles don't function to their full potential unless they have been stretched, neither do our spiritual muscles ever see their full potential unless we are in situations which stretch us. This is why Paul intentionally uses the word 'training' to describe how Timothy should develop – 'train yourself to be godly'.

Praying verses of Scripture repeatedly can be helpful here. For example:

'You will not succeed by your own strength or power, but by my Spirit,' says the LORD All-Powerful.'
(Zechariah 4:6)

You could build a routine using different topics, whereby you pray for your job environment when stretching your neck muscles, your family environment when stretching your back etc.

Andy Flannagan, *God 360°*, Spring Harvest & Authentic, 2006

Reaction Reaction Reaction Reaction

CIRCLE:

☺ ☹ 😐 ‼ 😕 😮

TICK:

Total rubbish ☐ Not sure ☐ Worth thinking about ☐ Genius ☐

FILL:

....

....

....

....

....

Soul

Your identity

'Before I made you in your mother's womb, I chose you. Before you were born, I set you apart for a special work. I appointed you as a prophet to the nations.'

(Jeremiah 1:5)

First up

We're going to ask you a really simple question:

Who are you?

Take a moment to think about it.

We're not asking what you do, or where you are from, or who your family are, or what you like doing, or what you look like, we are asking who are you? Most of the time when people ask who we are, we tell them what we do: 'I'm a scientist' or 'I'm a student studying for my GCSEs' or 'I'm a good guitarist' and so on. If we're pressed further, we might go on to say 'I'm a Geordie', or an 'American', or 'I'm a Manchester City supporter', or 'I'm John and Mary's son'. Actually, all those answers are about what we do or where we're from.

Our identity, the essence of who we are, is something deeper than that. It's the thing that you would still be even if everything else was stripped away. Think about it. If you were locked up in prison in a remote jungle and you no longer had contact with anyone or anything you currently know, what would be left, who would you be? That is your identity, the thing that's left after you set aside everything you do, think and relate to. It's who God made you.

Many people who aren't Christians spend years trying to 'find themselves', working out who they really are. Why? Because they've realised that there must be more to them than what they do, or who they are related to. However, without knowledge of their identity in Christ they wander round unable to find answers to their deepest questions. As Christians, we need to know our identity in God, we need to learn what he says about us and believe it. Only by being secure in our own identity can we bring hope to a world that has hopelessly lost its identity and is trying to find it through looks, things and activities.

So what is your identity in Christ? Read the verse at the start of this lesson and rewrite it in your own words with your name in it below.

Identity

Case one: A case of mistaken identity

My family was always one of the last to leave church after the Sunday service was over. For my sister and me, these often proved to be difficult times, waiting around while our grown-up parents stood there speaking in their grown-up language to other grown-ups. How thoroughly boring. All we wanted to do was go home. Once, out of pure desperation, I ran up to my mom, let out a massive sigh and threw my arms around her waist. 'Hello there Chip'. It wasn't my mother's voice. It wasn't my mother! I'd just desperately thrown my arms around the waist of the lady who lived next door to us. I slowly walked away to the sound of her grown-up friends' laughter. As my cheeks turned red, she very sweetly called out, 'I love you too!'

Many people find their own identity in the things people say about them. 'This is Susie, she's a dancer', or 'This is Robert, and he's rubbish at cooking.' Others find their identity from what the media says about their *kind*. That's why there are so many different magazines out there, offering advice and opinions to whatever kind of people they're targeting. Still others find their identity in the things they love to do. Ever heard the phrase, 'You are what you eat', or 'You are what you worship'? Some people are absolutely mad about shopping; others can't seem to get enough of sport. Their identity is wrapped up in whatever they give most of their time to.

Case two: A case of true identity

When we begin to look at the Bible, we find that God has an entirely different identity for us than what the world tries to offer. We start to understand that, actually, we're citizens of heaven, only visiting this planet for a brief vapour of time.

As you read God's Word today, take time to concentrate on what he says about you, because there you'll find your true identity.

God's mind

But you are a chosen people, royal priests, a holy nation, a people for God's own possession. You were chosen to tell about the wonderful acts of God, who called you out of darkness into his wonderful light. At one time you were not a people, but now you are God's people. In the past you had never received mercy, but now you have received God's mercy.

Dear friends, you are like foreigners and strangers in this world. I beg you to avoid the evil . . .
(1 Peter 2:9–11a)

Think only about the things in heaven, not the things on earth. Your old sinful self has died, and your new life is kept with Christ in God. Christ is our life, and when he comes again, you will share in his glory.
(Colossians 3:2–4)

But our homeland is in heaven, and we are waiting for our Saviour, the Lord Jesus Christ, to come from heaven. By his power to rule all things, he will change our simple bodies and make them like his own glorious body.
(Philippians 3:20,21)

Then you will be innocent and without any wrong. You will be God's children without fault. But you are living with crooked and evil people all around you, among whom you shine like stars in the dark world.

(Philippians 2:15)

Your mind

When was the last time I experienced a case of mistaken identity?

How would my best friend describe me?

Which activities do I most identify with?

What have I learned from the Bible that God says about me?

Chip Kendall, *The Mind Of ChipK: Enter At Your Own Risk*, Authentic, 2005

Hidden pearls

'Possibly in our day, young people were attracted to a famous speaker but you mustn't base yourself on someone else, even other Christians. You've got to be yourself and pray to God that he'll lead you into choosing your own identity. You've got to sort it out between you and God.'

Reaction Reaction Reaction Reaction

CIRCLE:

☺ ☹ 😐 ‼ 😕 😲

TICK:

Total rubbish ☐   Not sure ☐   Worth thinking about ☐   Genius ☐

FILL:

....

....

....

....

....

Name: **Katie Taylor**

Town: **Nottingham**

Age: **13**

Current status: **Lead singer in 3 bands**

What would you say to someone who is struggling with identity issues?

I'd tell them to stop following people, and give up on cliques. I'd tell them to be themselves. There's no point in copying people.

Do you know anyone who struggles with that?

Yeah.

Why do you think they struggle?

Because they just want to fit in. I know a lot of people that don't want to follow God because they think that people just won't accept them any more.

How has God spoken to you recently?

I was in a prayer room and this girl came up to me and told me that God had given her a picture of a stream with pebbles in it, and there was water and a gold ring. The water was pushing the pebbles along, and the gold ring didn't move.

What do you think that means?

I honestly have no idea, but I believe it was from God.

MOVE OVER
Mona Lisa

Bible reading: Ephesians 2:4–10

For we are God's masterpiece

(Ephesians 2:10, NLT)

You don't hang on the wall. You don't stand frozen like a carved-up rock. Yet you are God's masterpiece. More stunning than the most ornate sculpture or the most sublime painting, you are God's cherished, hand-crafted creation. Look at what Ephesians 2 says about your worth and value:

• You are alive together with Christ (verse 5).

• You were raised up with Christ (verse 6).

• You are now seated with Christ in heaven (verse 6).

• You are one with Christ Jesus (verse 6).

• You have been saved by God's special favour (verse 8).

And that's only the beginning. If you have trusted Christ, every one of the following huge truths is a fact about you. Whenever you wonder if you matter to God or anyone else, read this list aloud to yourself:

• I have peace with God (Romans 5:1).

• I am loved and chosen by God (Ephesians 1:4).

• I am a child of God (John 1:12).

• God's Holy Spirit lives in me (1 Corinthians 3:16).

• I have access to God's wisdom (James 1:5).

• I am helped by God (Hebrews 4:16).

• I have been reconciled to God (Romans 5:11).

• I am not condemned (Romans 8:1).

• I have been made right with God (Romans 5:1).

• I have Christ's righteousness (2 Corinthians 5:21).

- I am God's ambassador (2 Corinthians 5:20).
- I am completely forgiven (Colossians 1:14).
- God meets all my needs (Philippians 4:19)
- I am tenderly loved by God (Jeremiah 31:3)
- I am holy and blameless (Colossians 1:22).

Paul meant it when he said, 'If anyone belongs to Christ, there begins a new creation. The old things have gone: everything is made new!' (2 Corinthians 5:17). When God looks at you, he sees his flawless and awesome masterpiece.

REFLECT: DO YOU BELIEVE THAT YOU ARE GOD'S MASTERPIECE? SPEND TIME CHEWING ON ANY OF THOSE BIBLE FACTS ABOUT YOU THAT YOU HAVE A HARD TIME SWALLOWING.

PRAY: THANK GOD FOR HIS GREAT LOVE FOR YOU.

Josh McDowell, *Youth Devotions 2*, Tyndale House, 2003

Reaction Reaction Reaction Reaction

CIRCLE:

TICK:

Total rubbish ☐   Not sure ☐   Worth thinking about ☐   Genius ☐

FILL:

....

....

....

....

....

Who chose whom?

Grab your TV remote control. Flick around your channels or Teletext pages for a few minutes. Exercise your 'right' to choose. Now read John 15:9–17.

With regard to choice, we seem to live in a paradox. We make so many choices every day that we begin to believe that our choice to follow God is just another of those choices. It is the inevitable product of a consumer society which champions choice as a virtue and an economic driver. Yet we who choose so independently still desperately desire to be chosen, to be selected, to be picked out. We still have memories of being the last one standing when school teams were picked, or of the first time a boy asked us to dance. **FEELING CHOSEN IS INTENSELY IMPORTANT TO US.** Into this paradox steps Jesus with 'You did not choose me, I chose you' (John 15:16), but to see the depth of this we need some context.

In Rob Bell's book, *Velvet Elvis* (Grand Rapids, Zondervan, 2005), he describes how only the best of the best of young Jewish scholars would make it through the various levels of Hebrew education to the point where they could ask for an interview with a rabbi. During this interview, the rabbi would discern if they had what it took to be one of his select followers. So you can see what a world-inverting experience it would have been for some uneducated fishermen to have a rabbi walk straight up to them and inform them that he is choosing them.

Do you respond best to blanket instructions aimed at a large group or to a personal phone call commissioning you to do a specific task? I suspect we all operate better when we know we are doing a job we have been individually asked to do. There is a conferred sense of status and identity. Can you hear the call? Can you believe he has selected you? Because '**MANY PEOPLE ARE INVITED, BUT ONLY A FEW ARE CHOSEN**' (Matthew 22:14) and 'the gate is small and the road is narrow that leads to true life. Only a few people find that road' (Matthew 7:14).

And notice the authority that comes with being chosen – 'This is my Son whom I have chosen. Listen to him' (Luke 9:35). This is the Father speaking publicly about Jesus during the multimedia spectacle we sometimes call the transfiguration. Jesus is God, yet the Father is underlining the amazing truth that Jesus is chosen, so perhaps we need to know it too. At our core.

There is a song called 'All I Am' by a dodgy Irish singer-songwriter called Andy Flannagan. It contains the words 'I am broken, but I am chosen, for you have spoken grace to me.' You could meditate on or sing these words until they sink in beyond your mind and to your heart.

Andy Flannagan, *God 360°*, Spring Harvest & Authentic, 2006

Reaction Reaction Reaction Reaction

CIRCLE:

☺ ☹ 😐 😮 😕 😲

TICK:

Total rubbish ☐   Not sure ☐   Worth thinking about ☐   Genius ☐

FILL:

....
....
....
....
....

WHOSE PORTRAIT IS THIS?

Chip talks

Sometimes Jesus did some pretty strange things. He walked on water. He slept through a storm at sea. He even healed a man's eyes by rubbing them with a mixture of mud and his own saliva. Weird. So why did he choose to act in such an unorthodox manner? Was he trying to think outside the box? Was he making sure the people around him wouldn't forget what he was about to do? Was he simply following exact instructions given to him by his Father in heaven? It was probably a mixture of all these things and more.

In Mark 12:13–17, Jesus does one such peculiar thing. There were some dodgy people trying to trick him into saying something that would get him into big trouble. They asked Jesus if it was right to pay taxes to Caesar (the ruling Roman emperor). He responded by having

someone to bring him a coin. Then, referring to the coin, he asked, 'Whose image and name are on the coin?' They answered, 'Caesar's.' Then Jesus said to them, **'GIVE TO CAESAR THE THINGS THAT ARE CAESAR'S AND GIVE TO GOD THE THINGS THAT ARE GOD'S.'** Whoa. Pretty deep answer if you ask me. He had them well and truly stumped.

I believe this particular passage is talking about a lot more than just paying taxes. He was also talking about identity. When Jesus said, 'Give to God the things that are God's,' he may have been referring to the fact that all of us have been made in the image of God. This is something we're taught right at the start of the Bible, in Genesis, where Adam and Eve are made in God's image. He breathes life into them. In Hebrew, the word for breath is also the word for spirit. So part of being made in God's image is having a spirit – just like him. And that means our identity must always be wrapped in God.

So the next time you look at yourself in the mirror, why not try doing something strange and peculiar? Ask yourself this question: 'Whose portrait is this? And whose inscription?' Once you've come up with the answer, remember the words of Jesus: 'Give to God the things that are God's.'

> So brothers and sisters, since God has shown us great mercy, I beg you to offer your lives as a living sacrifice to him. Your offering must be only for God and pleasing to him, which is the spiritual way for you to worship.

(Romans 12:1)

Reaction Reaction Reaction Reaction

CIRCLE:

TICK:

Total rubbish ☐   Not sure ☐   Worth thinking about ☐   Genius ☐

FILL:

....

....

....

....

....

Woman of God

Helen talks

Girls, have you ever wondered what a woman of God looks like?
Is she some wild-eyed prophetess with a long flowing skirt?
Is she a missionary dressed in rags and working in a remote jungle?
Is she a boffin with big glasses who sits reading the Bible all day?
No. She looks like YOU.

Women of God come in all shapes and sizes, the point is they are people who have given their lives to God and are secure in a few important truths. They regularly say sorry to God for the stuff they do wrong and know that they are forgiven. They live life secure in the knowledge that God sees them through Jesus and what he did on the cross. He sees them as they will be, not just as they are. They spend their lives trying to become that person God has saved them to be.

They are secure in the fact that God didn't make any mistakes when he made them. They've had enough of petty comparisons with others and they are happy to get on with the job God has given them to do. Check out this amazing verse below. This is truth, and it's talking about you:

You made my whole being; you formed me in my mother's body.
I praise you because you made me in an amazing and wonderful way. What you have done is wonderful. I know this very well.
You saw my bones being formed as I took shape in my mother's body. When I was put together there, you saw my body as it was formed. All the days planned for me were written in your book before I was one day old.

(Psalm 139:13–16)

She is also a woman of action, she's not somebody who floats through life on some kind of super-spiritual cloud, **SHE'S GOT HER HEAD SCREWED ON** and she's working hard at serving God and others. Proverbs 31:10–31 gives the Bible's take on what a good wife is like, I think you can apply these guidelines to being a godly woman, whether you are married or not. You can read it for yourself but here are some of the things the passage says about her:

- Trustworthy
- A good business woman
- Provides for people
- Works hard
- Strong
- Knows what she's good at
- Helps the poor and needy
- Wears good clothes
- Respected
- Excited about the future
- Wise
- Kind
- Doesn't waste time
- Gets her reward
- Respects God

You have the potential to be an amazing, godly woman, a role model for others around you and someone who can change the world in some way. Ask God what areas of your life need work; ask him to help you become more of the woman of God he has made you to be.

First up

SELF-ESTEEM

God has made us what we are. In Christ Jesus, God made us to do good works, which God planned in advance for us to live our lives doing.

(Ephesians 2:10)

According to the Oxford English dictionary, self-esteem means 'confidence in one's own worth or abilities'. Some people you know might have way too much confidence in their own worth and abilities, they think they are the best thing ever and that they know everything. Others may have very little confidence in their own worth, or may even think they are worthless. And some people may have a fairly good balance between those two extremes. In this section, hopefully you will be able to figure out where you fit in that spectrum. Do you think too much of yourself, or not enough? As we've already learned, God has some amazing things to say about you so if you feel worthless you need to work towards believing some of the things God said are true about you, too. This can be easier said than done, but hopefully some of the extracts coming up can help. Having a well-balanced sense of self-esteem is really important to get and really hard to find as you are growing up. As you get older, a lack of confidence could hold you back from achieving your potential, where as over confidence or arrogance may discourage people from working with you. With so many voices shouting at you, trying to tell you what a young person should be like, it can be very hard to get a good self-image so take your time with this, really think about what you are reading and how it applies to you. Hopefully, this will help you grow up with a balanced sense of who you are.

Rewrite the verse from Ephesians above in your own words:

How does that make you feel about yourself?

Reality Check

HOW HEALTHY IS *YOUR* SELF-IMAGE?

Circle one answer for each question then use the table at the end to add up your score.

1. When you look in the mirror do you think:

a Oh my goodness what a disaster area, pass the paper bag

b Not too bad, maybe shower and shave/makeup would help

c My gosh, I am the best looking person I've seen in ages. Check me out!

2. When you do something well do you think:

a It's nothing new, I do everything well

b Well, it was good but probably only because others helped

c No matter what people say, it probably wasn't any good anyway

3. When you receive a compliment about something do you:

a Ignore it – clearly they don't know what they are talking about

b Accept it and feel pleased, but try not to get a big head

c Realise it just confirms what you already knew about yourself

4. When you do something wrong, do you think:

a Oh well, I can learn from this and do better next time

b How predictable, it just proves how stupid I am

c How ridiculous, it was someone else's fault it went wrong, not mine

5. When you are accused of something you didn't do, do you:

a Make it known to everyone around that you didn't do it and slate the person accusing you for good measure

b Keep quiet, you probably deserved it anyway

c Have a quiet word with the person accusing you and then trust that people who know you will not listen to the gossip

6. When you are praised for something you didn't do, do you:

a Take the praise and enjoy it – you probably deserved it anyway

b Don't get stressed about it, instead have a quiet word with the appropriate people and explain that in fact it wasn't you

c Feel absolutely mortified and rush around explaining that it wasn't you

ANALYSIS

Add up your score

Question 1	A = 3	B = 2	C = 1
Question 2	A = 1	B = 2	C = 3
Question 3	A = 3	B = 2	C = 1
Question 4	A = 2	B = 3	C = 1
Question 5	A = 1	B = 3	C = 2
Question 6	A = 1	B = 2	C = 3

Total score

Low score (6–9)

You have very high self-esteem and a lot of confidence. That is a really good thing. It's good to be proud of who you are and confident in your abilities and talents. However, perhaps sometimes you have a tendency to be big headed and trample over other people's feelings. Make sure you balance that confidence with humility and a servant attitude.

Medium score (10–14)

You seem to have a fairly balanced sense of self-esteem. You are quietly confident but don't rub other people's faces in it. Perhaps you sometimes don't take credit for your good work but don't be afraid to do this. When you do well at something celebrate it, God has given you talents and abilities that no one else has.

High score (15–18)

You seem to have really low self-esteem and you may lack confidence. Remember and believe that God made you just the way he wanted you. You are no accident, you are unique and have a role to lead that no one else has. Please talk to someone about how you feel, it may feel like you are the only one, but many, many people struggle with low self-esteem. It's possible that you are struggling with eating problems or self-harm, find someone you trust and ask them for help.

DO YOURSELF A FAVOUR
and love yourself

Read Matthew 22:34–40

Love your neighbour as you love yourself.
(Matthew 22:39)

They're out there. They think you don't see them. But you do. And it makes you gag. Unless you happen to be one of them . . .

- A guy struts in front of a locker room mirror and flexes and poses like he's Mr World Champion Body Builder.

- A girl pauses to admire herself in a shopping mall window. She fluffs her hair, then lays a lip print on her reflection.

- A guy won't shut up about how great and tough he is.

- A girl splashes her bedroom wall with blown up photos of herself, modelling all her outfits.

When the Bible commands you to love others like you love yourself, that's not exactly what God meant. Yes, there's a healthy kind of self-love, but bragging about your greatness or being infatuated with your looks is conceit, not love.

Matthew 22:39 implies that you won't love others in the right way unless you can love yourself in the right way. Is that OK? Look at it this way: God loves you, so you can love yourself. God accepts you, so you can accept yourself. God cherishes you as his unique creation, so you can cherish yourself. Liking yourself like that isn't just OK, it's great. It's what God wants.

SEEING YOURSELF AS GOD SEES YOU – NO MORE OR NO LESS – IS A HEALTHY SELF-IMAGE. That's an uplifting thing. It's also a humbling thing – because you recognise that every gift you possess comes from the Lord Jesus Christ.

Another kind of self-image is unhealthy. An unhealthy self-image can be either negative or positive. People with a negative self-image get down on themselves. People with a positive self-image get high on themselves. What warps these two views is their reliance on the world's systems of value and worth – that what matters most about you is your looks, abilities, intelligence, possessions, etc. When you think well of yourself based on the world's standards, you easily slide into pride.

You can be sure you're loving yourself in the right way when you love others more as a result. And when you make loving others your goal, everything then falls into place. Life – and liking yourself – makes sense. You put others, beginning with Christ, smack in the centre of your attention. And when that happens, God is pleased.

REFLECT: DESCRIBE IN YOUR OWN WORDS A HEALTHY SELF-IMAGE.

PRAY: FATHER, TEACH ME TO LOVE MYSELF IN THE RIGHT WAY SO I'LL LOVE OTHERS AS A RESULT.

Josh McDowell, *Youth Devotions 2*, Tyndale House, 2003

Reaction Reaction Reaction Reaction

CIRCLE:

TICK:

Total rubbish ☐   Not sure ☐   Worth thinking about ☐   Genius ☐

FILL:

....

....

Popular

Many of today's big political speeches are tested on focus groups to ascertain which sections are making the listeners 'feel good'. Phrases are edited or removed if they don't meet with high percentage approval. About 2,000 years ago on a hillside, a man delivered a speech that would have failed almost every test that a pollster could throw at it. Towards the end of it, he challenges a lot of assumptions and 'raises the bar' beyond where any of his listeners would have been comfortable. I can imagine the slashes of red pen his spin doctors would have put throughout the text. 'You can't say that.'

Read Matthew chapter 5. Read it as a speech, as that is what it was. You could shoot a video of yourself delivering it, then watch it back.

Let's face it. Most of us are people-pleasers. We care more about what people think of us than perhaps anything else. Our credibility and image are like strait-jackets preventing us from challenging the status quo. **HOW DO WE CHANGE FROM BEING PEOPLE-PLEASERS TO GOD-PLEASERS?**

Analyse the decisions you make today, and assess what part pleasing people had in those decisions. When did we make that journey that all children seem to make from wanting to please our fathers and mothers, to caring more about pleasing our peers? Is it fear of people, is it fear of conflict, is it a desire to be popular? Reflect on how little these factors impacted Jesus' life. He never sought human approval, checking for applause after a miracle, or scavenging through email feedback for affirmation. However, the journey should not end with the phrase 'God-pleaser'. We can seek God's approval just as unhealthily as we seek other people's. Jesus was never seeking his Father's approval through his ministry. He knew that he had it. Let the truth that you don't have to work for his approval rise above any other temptation to go looking for it from others.

Another example of people-pleasing taking second place in the Bible is when Peter and John were called before the Sanhedrin, and received some seemingly absolute news in Acts 4:18. 'So they called Peter and John in again and told them not to speak or teach at all in the name of Jesus.'

Peter and John take absolutely no heed of this edict, even though there were many practical reasons why it would have been a good idea. When they are hauled back in, Acts 5:29 sums up their reply. **'WE MUST OBEY GOD, NOT HUMAN AUTHORITY!'**

Make a list of 'false absolutes' like this, that you have begun to believe, that prevent you speaking or acting as you are called. Examples could be – 'It's unprofessional to mention your faith at work.' 'People don't want leadership any more.'

Bring before God the decisions you make today, and your honest assessment of them, regarding people-pleasing. Ask that he would give you the strength to make that journey from people-pleasing to God-fearing.

Andy Flannagan, *God 360°*, Spring Harvest & Authentic, 2006

Reaction Reaction Reaction Reaction

CIRCLE:

TICK:

Total rubbish ☐   Not sure ☐   Worth thinking about ☐   Genius ☐

FILL:

....

....

....

....

....

Name: **Daniel Butchers**

Town: **Salisbury**

Age: **18**

Current status: **Training to be a life guard, but can't go swimming for a while due to an ear operation.**

When do you think Jesus is coming back?

I don't know. Years, hopefully, because I don't want to be alive when he does, because there's going to be a lot of chaos, and I want to have a nice long life.

What do you want to get done before Jesus comes back?

Clean up the world a bit and try and stop racism. That's one thing I really don't like.

What would be your advice to someone who's struggling with identity issues?

Just be yourself and get as much confidence as you can, because the reason a lot of people have identity issues is because they're not confident in themselves. Once you've got your confidence sorted out, I've found that the rest just fits into place.

How did you struggle with confidence?

I was picked on a little bit at school because I was dyslexic and that really knocked my confidence back.

What helped you get over it?

Just being with God and talking to him and having friends that I found were very like me instead of me trying to be like them.

GUESS WHAT I HEARD ABOUT YOU?

Read Proverbs 19:19–23

Listen to advice and accept correction, and in the end you will be wise.

(Proverbs 19:20)

You tell your friend you signed up for the football team. 'Are you kidding?' he snorts. **'THE ONLY POSITION THE COACH WILL LET YOU PLAY IS LEFT END – *OF THE BENCH!*'**

You come home and announce that you're trying out for the chorus in your school's spring drama production. Your older sister scowls. 'Why are you doing that? **YOU COULDN'T CARRY A TUNE IF IT CAME IN A BUCKET.'**

You walk into a party proud of your new outfit. Two students eye you up and down. You hear one of them say, **'SHE ALWAYS WEARS CHEAP OUTFITS.'**

Criticism stings. And if you don't deal with the hurt you feel, it makes your self-image stink. No one escapes getting stung by others. But with God's help you can take the unkind words of others as opportunities to become wise. Here's how.

First, decide if the criticism is deserved. If it is, you have something to work on. Sometimes criticism is what it takes to make us correct flaws, change motivations, and learn to be sensitive to others.

Second, sometimes your critic was honestly trying to help, so say thanks for the input. But it won't help anyone if you sass something like, 'Thanks. I so very much value the opinion of a jerk like you.'

Third, remember who you are – God's much-loved child. You are valued, accepted and gifted. Don't let the criticism damage that view of yourself. So what do you do when someone compliments you? It's easy to go to one of two extremes. One extreme? False humility. You deny any positive quality of accomplishment by saying something like, 'No, no, no. I'm just a dung-burrowing worm.' That makes people sick. Everyone knows that inside you're screaming, 'Say it again! Tell me again how great I am!'

The other extreme is to agree with the person who compliments you to the point of bragging. You know people like that. You say one nice thing and they remind you of twenty other things they do well.

When you get a compliment, first see if it is deserved. If it isn't, pass the credit on to someone else. If it is, simply say, 'Thank you.'

For every compliment, whisper a thanks to Jesus. After all, he is the source of your gifts, abilities, looks and personality. If you hold on to the compliments instead of giving credit to God, you forget that he is your source and you start believing that you're the source. That's pride.

REFLECT: HAVE YOU BEEN CRITICISED OR COMPLIMENTED RECENTLY? HOW DID YOU REACT?

PRAY: ASK GOD TO HELP YOU RECEIVE CRITICISM AND COMPLIMENTS WITH GRACE.

Josh McDowell, *Youth Devotions 2*, Tyndale House, 2003

ReactionReactionReactionReaction

CIRCLE:

TICK:

Total rubbish ☐   Not sure ☐   Worth thinking about ☐   Genius ☐

FILL:

....

....

....

....

....

First up

In this section we are going to look at some of the ways people deal with hurt and pain in their lives: eating disorders and self-harming. These problems have many deep causes but both are linked with and cause very low self-esteem. These two struggles may not apply to you — it is possible to have low self-esteem without having these problems — so we will look at other issues related to low self-esteem later in this book. However, if you think you are struggling with one or both of these problems, the following extracts will give you a bit of info about them. It would be impossible to put enough information to completely help you in this small book so we really recommend that you talk to someone you trust about your problems. An older Christian would be a really good idea. Also, there are some great books out in Christian book stores that give more help and advice. Please check them out, too. Remember these aren't problems to be ashamed of and you are not the only one who is facing them. Talk to someone and get help. If you are struggling, you may find these extracts and stories difficult to read. Before you start, pray that God will help you to hear what the writers are saying and apply it to your life.

EATING DISORDERS

In her excellent book on overcoming eating disorders (*Hidden Hunger*, Authentic, 2004), Maxine Vorster gives the following descriptions of three eating disorders.

Anorexia Nervosa – Anorexia is usually defined as a deliberate and excessive starvation in the pursuit of thinness.

Bulimia – This is a pattern of recurring episodes of swinging between binge eating – which means eating lots of food in a short space of time, and forced elimination – which means making yourself sick.

Compulsive over eating – More than the occasional over-indulgence, this is an uncontrollable consumption of large amounts of food that is not based on hunger.

An eating disorder is basically when you have any kind of unhealthy relationship with food. Although there are some websites and magazines that encourage these disorders, please remember that they are dangerous and will hurt you emotionally, spiritually and physically. We don't have space to deal with eating disorders in detail but if you are struggling please get help. We really recommend you read *Hidden Hunger* by Maxine Vorster which goes into much more depth than we can here. Here are two stories of people with eating disorders and how it affected their lives:

The way God changed my life

During this whole time [at school], I felt so rubbish about myself. I looked in the mirror and felt ugly, worthless and insecure. All I wanted was for someone to love me. All of these feelings made me so confused. I longed to fit in with everyone else but I didn't know what else to do. I so desperately wanted to be in control of my own life that in order to be in control of something, I stopped eating. Eating was the one thing that I had total control of. No one could make me eat if I didn't want to.

For 3 months all I ate was chewing gum and drank cups of tea. I used to go down for breakfast earlier than everyone else and swish Weetabix round in a bowl, pour it down the sink and leave my bowl out so that it looked like I had eaten something. I used to take a packed lunch to school and throw it in the bin as soon as I got there so that even if I felt hungry, I wouldn't have anything to eat when it came to lunch time. I used to lie constantly to my mum and dad. I would tell them anything as long as it meant I didn't have to eat any dinner. Something that I started off in control of became in control of me.

After a few months, my parents found out that I hadn't been eating anything and dragged me to the doctor. I was convinced that there was nothing wrong with me. I went into the doctor's kicking and screaming. The doctor took one look at me and said that I had an eating disorder called Anorexia Nervosa. I weighted 6 1/2 stone, my periods had virtually stopped, I had skin problems because of not having any vitamins, I was constantly exhausted and to top it all off, I was told that unless I started eating again I only had 8 weeks to live. I looked over to my mum and dad and saw the disappointment in their eyes. They had just been told that their daughter could die. I will never understand what it was like for them to have to go through that.

I had come to a point in my life where I had a huge decision to make. Was I going to carry on not eating and eventually starve myself to death or was I going to do something about this mess I had landed myself in? I had tried to get help from my friends and family but no one seemed to be able to understand what I was feeling. But I remembered what Steve, Jon and Tim had told me about God and the fact that even if I didn't love him, he loved me no matter what. I didn't know if I believed in God or not but I knew that I didn't have any other options left, so I prayed and asked God to help me. I said, 'Alright God, if you really love me as much as you say you do, come and help me out of this mess.' There was no immediate difference but I somehow knew that God was there. I started going to church and reading my Bible and finding out more about God.

When I was first diagnosed with Anorexia, the doctors told me that I would never really get over it. They said that once you've had an eating disorder you never fully recover. The thing they didn't realise was that I had God on my side! Within 2 years, God had completely healed me! I had endless sessions of counselling at the hospital that did help a little bit, but the biggest influence was undoubtedly God. It was as if I was a brand new person. God totally transformed me inside and out and made me whole again by simply loving me. Come on now, that's what I call a miracle.

Shell Perris, *Something to Shout About*, **Authentic, 2006**

Caroline Bone's testimony

I started to struggle with an eating disorder when I was in my mid-twenties. My parents divorced when I was nineteen and my father died a few years later. Pressures at work and home were growing and I felt like food was my only comfort and friend. I would eat large quantities of food at one time and keep food hidden away in my room. Later, though, I began to panic about putting on weight and would try to make myself sick – fortunately I did not succeed and consequently concluded I did not have a problem. I was in denial.

About 4 years later, whilst living in Canada, attending the School of Ministry, I was in the café one day and bought some sweets. I quickly put them into my pocket so that no one else would see. As I did, I felt the Holy Spirit stop me in my tracks, saying? 'What are you doing?' I could deny it no longer – food had a hold on my life. I spoke with one of the staff and they prayed for me and I agreed to be accountable to them. I realised that I was allowing food to be my comforter rather than God.

Over the previous months God had been teaching me what it meant to be fathered by him and how little I understood about what that meant because, like most fathers, mine wasn't perfect. One particular area I struggled with was trying to live up to my father's expectations and constantly feeling like I failed. My dad found it very difficult to show me his love, which also added to my feelings of worthlessness.

I had to deal with these and many other issues in my life, learning to forgive those who had hurt me and repent of my own sinful actions. As I did this more and more I was able to know God's love for me and feel secure in that love. The food issue was out in the open but I had my good days and my bad days and I still didn't feel in control. Finally the day came when I had had enough and I told God I was willing to give up my right to use food as a comfort, asking him to set me free. The two people who were with me when I came to this point prayed for me and I was set free from a spirit of addiction.

Now I was free to choose the way I used food – but I emphasise 'choose'. I felt very different after that prayer but times of testing still came. When my world was shaken by circumstances outside my control I had to choose to ask God to help me and allow him to be my comfort instead of food. The more I did this the more I found that God was a far better comforter!

Maxine Vorster, *Hidden Hunger*, Authentic, 2006

Reaction Reaction Reaction Reaction

CIRCLE:

TICK:

Total rubbish ☐   Not sure ☐   Worth thinking about ☐   Genius ☐

FILL:

....

....

SELF-HARM

What is self-harm?

Self-harm is a deliberate, immediate physical act of harm against yourself. If you are not a self-harmer you may want to ask, 'Why would anyone choose to inflict pain on themselves? It just doesn't make any sense.' Well, you have a point.

But to someone who has got into the habit of self-harming, their behaviour is not irrational or senseless. People often hurt themselves to try and feel better, not worse. Just like someone who smokes: they don't see their behaviour as senseless or destructive – even though many others would disagree.

Sometimes people do things that make sense to them but not to anyone else. You may well know someone who has walked out on a 'happy' marriage. It doesn't make sense to anyone else, but to them it feels as though it is the only option. Those who self-harm can feel this way too. They can feel trapped by their patterns of thinking and behaviour.

If you are such a person, then we pray that by reading this you will think things through in a new way. Self-harm is cruel, crude and destructive (this you know). The prospect of giving it up may feel a total impossibility. You may never have even admitted that you are someone who society would call a 'self-harmer'. We need you to know that **SELF-HARM IS NOT THE ONLY OR THE BEST WAY OF COPING** with how you feel. For many people who have self-harmed, there comes a moment of breakthrough, a moment when they realise that there is a way out. Our prayer is that you will be brought nearer to that moment for yourself. May God richly bless your mind and your body as you read these words.

You may be going through something really tough at the moment – deep trouble at home or school, or maybe even both. It may even be hard to read these words because you are aching inside. You may feel so lonely that you are driven to anger and frustration – or beyond it. But hope and help are not as far away as you feel.

There are all sorts of negative things that people do when they get stressed or worried. Some people hurt themselves because they see others doing it and think it may be the only way to cope with feelings of anger and hurt. The problem with this is that it can leave them feeling worse. Maybe you are angry or anxious, so you want to lash out in some way. You might feel alone, or neglected, as if no one is really there for you. It could be that you are incredibly tense and want a way out. You may not know why you are hurting yourself at all. Many people who suffer say that they can't pinpoint any particular emotion that triggers their harming.

Some people hurt themselves as a way of releasing tension or as an escape from life. People have said that they want to relieve anger and stress and cope with feelings of loneliness or depression. Everyone is different and so the reasons that people hurt themselves vary from person to person.

Self-harm may result from being told that the way a person is acting is wrong or inappropriate for some reason. Often the person feels less connected to the world than they were. Maybe something traumatic has happened which has made them feel shut off from others they once relied on.

Many people who self-harm have these things in common:

1. They are trying to cope with turbulent emotions.

2. They are trying to communicate things that they cannot say in words either to themselves and/or to others.

3. They are trying to take control over their bodies, sometimes by 'punishing themselves' to relieve overwhelming feelings.

Stopping harm

To stop hurting yourself is a very personal and hard decision, particularly if it's something you have relied on in the past to 'help you' feel better. We don't want to put you off sharing this with someone. But, if you do choose to tell someone like your youth leader or teacher about the fact that you are hurting yourself, remember this: they can't promise to keep what you've told them secret. This is to protect you and them. It isn't because they don't care about you or want to grass on you. It's because they want you to be kept safe. You may decide with them that someone else needs to help you through the situation. Maybe someone who knows more about things like this than they do.

If you know that you need to stop doing something that is destructive and damaging for you, here are some things that you can do to break the cycle. (These things are real ideas that people who have kicked the habit have done.)

1. Admit that you are self-harming.

2. Admit you want and need to stop.

3. Ask God in to the secret place of your heart.

4. Ask him to begin to change your attitudes and begin the healing process.

5. Choose someone you trust in your friends/family circle who will support you and pray with you.

6. Get at least two people you can call/txt at any time of day or night.

7. Write yourself a list of ten things you can do instead of harming.

8. Get rid of things that you have hurt yourself with, or are likely to use again (one girl actually found it useful to give them to her youth leader).

9. Find a safe and special place you can go in your house when you feel like harming.

10. Try not to give up, even if you slip up.

Breaking the cycle rarely happens first time – although there are some people who have been given the strength to stop once and for all, and never return to harming. You are the only person who can stop you harming yourself. You have to force yourself to try. It won't be easy but no one can do it for you.

Only you and God know how you feel right now. Even if you see no way out, there is one. You don't have to hurt yourself any longer. Remember that God delights in who you are. He loves you passionately with a love that cannot be measured or changed or spoilt. He thinks you are amazing. He understands that you don't love yourself the way he wants you to, but he wants you to learn.

Ems Hancock and Ian Henderson, *Sorted?*, Authentic, 2004

Reaction Reaction Reaction Reaction

CIRCLE:

😊 ☹️ 😐 😦 🙂 😮

TICK:

Total rubbish ☐ Not sure ☐ Worth thinking about ☐ Genius ☐

FILL:

....

....

....

....

....

Not quite good enough

Helen talks

'. . . no one is thinking about you, they're all thinking about themselves, just like you.'

(Helen Fielding, *Olivia Joules and the Overactive Imagination*, Picador, 2004)

I know there must be a lot of you out there who don't have eating disorders, or self-harm problems but you do go through life with the feeling that you are just not quite good enough. Not quite as clever as your sister, not quite as sporty as your friend, not quite as good looking as your best mate, not quite as fun as someone else in your youth group. There is always someone smarter, better looking, funnier, or whatever, than you. In life we can often be made to feel like we are too much or not enough. We are told to talk more because we are not chatty enough, or to be quiet because we are too loud, or to do more because we are too laid back, or to back off because we are too over the top. It seems impossible to get the balance just right. Some people seem to swan through life with a kind of inbuilt confidence, as if they always know the right decision to make, the right thing to say, or what to do next. For the rest of us, we go through life struggling with decisions, wondering if what we think is right, agonising over whether to reach out for opportunities where there is a chance we might fail.

When I was younger, I had fairly low self-esteem and a lack of confidence, although some people might not have known that. Among people I was comfortable with, I could be funny, chatty, confident but when I was with people I didn't know, or people I found intimidating, I was really quiet. I felt like I could never think of the right thing to say, or I didn't want to risk saying something wrong and everyone laughing at me. In fact, it was probably because I was worrying about it so much that I couldn't think of anything. What people thought of me was very important and in some ways I think I was a bit crippled by the fear of making a fool of myself.

As I've grown up, I have gained more experience which has meant that there are less and less people that I am intimidated by. I've realised that most people who seem really confident are actually insecure inside and that most of the time people aren't thinking about me as much as I think they are. I've become more confident in my abilities and my worth as a person through trying things and succeeding and through learning things.

I also know that the only reason I have grown in my self confidence is by following the path God has set before me. By stepping out and putting myself in uncomfortable situations I have grown, I have become more confident and my self-esteem has improved. If I had always let myself go and hide from difficult situations, I would still be the same as I was at 14. Now I am able to do a job that involves confronting people, meeting lots of new people and doing lots of things that I would have found difficult in the past. Sometimes when I do something wrong, or when I'm with new people that intimidate me, it all comes back and I realise that deep down some of those insecurities are still there. All I can do in those situations is pray that God will give me the guts to carry on regardless, to not run from my difficult things, but to confront them and grow.

In one of his songs, the singer Kevin Max says **'BE YOURSELF, THERE'S NO ONE CAN DO IT QUITE LIKE YOU . . . AND IF YOU DON'T THEN WHO IS GOING TO?'** I love that. What a good point. If I let my insecurities and low self-esteem get in the way of me accomplishing God's plan for my life, then it won't get done. No one else can do it quite like me. No one can do the job of being me, doing what I'm supposed to do, like me. That makes me feel like I have a responsibility to work through my issues and get on with the job. So whatever it takes, I would encourage you to improve your confidence and self-esteem. It may feel impossible but it's not. Pray to God, talk to someone you trust, see a counsellor, read some books, push yourself into uncomfortable situations and make it work.

Reaction Reaction Reaction Reaction

CIRCLE:

TICK:

Total rubbish ☐   Not sure ☐   Worth thinking about ☐   Genius ☐

FILL:

....

....

....

And the truth will set you free

One of the names given to Satan is the father of lies (see John 8:44). He lies all the time, especially to us and especially about who we are. He is our accuser – he condemns us before God, he desperately wants us to lose our way. A preacher once said that the devil's tactic used to be to kill Christians, so that they couldn't fight him. But he has discovered that it is far more effective to simply render them incapable of doing anything, by telling them lies. Sometimes Satan uses our insecurities: 'You're useless', 'You're ugly', 'You're stupid'. Other times he will attack us with pride; 'Well done me', 'I'm the best'. Neither reflect the identity we have in Christ. If we believe these thoughts that Satan puts our way then we are not living life in obedience to Christ. Satan's lies are the opposite of what God tells us about ourselves in the Bible.

There are amazing promises written about you in the Bible. God's Word to us is peppered with declarations about our identity, our purpose, our future and our relationship with our Creator. And yet so often we choose to ignore God's promises over us in favour of Satan's lies.

We fight with weapons that are different from those the world uses. Our weapons have power from God that can destroy the enemy's strong places. We destroy people's arguments and every proud thing that raises itself against the knowledge of God. We capture every thought and make it give up and obey Christ.
(2 Corinthians 10:4,5)

The actions you produce show the attitudes you have adopted. A friend of mine was constantly putting herself down. She didn't even notice that she was doing it half the time, 'Oh I couldn't do that', 'I don't deserve that opportunity, I'm not good enough', 'No one could like me, I'm ugly' and so it went on. Because of the lies, she never pushed herself forward, she was negative about herself and others, she grew depressed, and she became less and less like the person she actually was. Desperate to return to her true identity she began to fight the lies in her life. It took her a while but every time she noticed she was saying a lie about herself she refuted it. 'I am good enough "God has made us what we are. In Christ Jesus, God made us to do good works, which God planned in advance for us to live our lives doing."' (Ephesians 2:10). I'm not ugly, **"GOD LOOKED AT EVERYTHING HE HAD MADE, AND IT WAS VERY GOOD"**' (Genesis 1:31). Gradually, she started to live in confidence. She learnt who she was in Christ, to trust the promises she read in the Bible, and to recognise when Satan was trying to get her to stumble. The Word of God set her free. She was no longer held by the lies and curses she had spoken over herself, she was free to live in Christ.

Break the curse that you live under. Look at what the Bible says about you and then look at what you say about yourself. Which one should be brought into accordance with the other?

This Living Word is waiting for you. Read it. It is powerful against our enemies. It is foundational to our faith. There is nothing greater. There is nothing more precious than the gift of God's Word to us. Where you have found it dry or boring, ask God to breathe life into it. When you are rooted in his Word you will be rooted in him.

Andy Frost and Jo Wells, *Freestyle*, Authentic Media, 2005

ReactionReactionReactionReaction

CIRCLE:

TICK:

Total rubbish ☐   Not sure ☐   Worth thinking about ☐   Genius ☐

FILL:

....

....

....

Reality Check

MAINTAINING A HEALTHY SELF-IMAGE

Keeping a good sense of identity and self-image is all about knowing who you are and believing what God says about you. God made you unique, and it will help if you can stop comparing yourself to others all the time.

Read through some of the verses in the lessons you have already read.

Write down some truths about what the Bible says about your identity

I am...

I am ....

God has...

God will ....

NEGATIVE SPEAKING

Read through the list of words below and cross out any that you have heard coming out of your mouth about yourself. As you cross them out, make a decision not to say or think those things about yourself any more.

Ugly	Stupid	Fat	Lazy	Thick
Boring	Shy	Unfriendly	Undeserving	Inferior
Poor	Timid	Can't	Useless	Unplanned
Rubbish	Clumsy	Unlovable	Sinner	

(add more if you can think of any)

Read through the list of words below and tick any that you already say/think about yourself. Make a decision to declare these things over you and your life.

Important	Useful	Skilled	Individual	Special
Planned	Beautiful	Smart	Useful	Blessed
Interesting	Bold	Confident	Deserving	Loved
Saved	Chosen	Holy	Royal	

Now think about negative things that have been spoken over you by others (especially influential others such as family members, teachers, friends, etc.)

....

....

....

....

As you cross out any words like these that have been spoken over you, pray that God will help you to forgive the people who said these things and forget these negative words. It can be very hard to get out from under the influence of words that have been spoken over us so if you need to pray with someone about these things then please do. Talking to someone will also help you realise that you are none of these things.

Finally, fill in the blank and declare this statement over yourself, read it out loud (shout it if you can) and most of all believe it. It's true!

I, ... (your name), am made in the image of God, a God who loves me so much that he watched over me even when I was being formed in the womb. He made me just the way he wanted me to be. He gave me a unique blend of talents, abilities and personality traits that no one else has but me. He has planned out a course for me that no one else can follow and that no one else can do as well as me. I am fearfully and wonderfully made, loved and cherished by a perfect, enormous, powerful, holy God. Thank you Lord for making me me!

Spirit

Who are you going to be?

Remember the LORD in all you do,
and he will give you success.

(Proverbs 3:6)

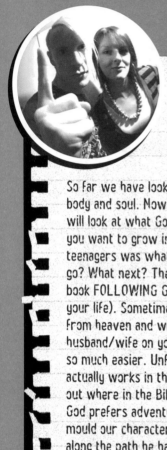

First up

Who are you going to be?

So far we have looked at two of the three things of our make up: body and soul. Now we are going to look at the third one: spirit. We will look at what God has called you to be and the kind of person you want to grow into. One of the main things we thought about as teenagers was what to do after finishing school, where should we go? What next? These are really hard questions (check out our book FOLLOWING GOD for more about finding God's direction for your life). Sometimes you can wish a giant hand would come down from heaven and write your future career and the name of your husband/wife on your bedroom wall for you, that way it would be so much easier. Unfortunately, it seems to be fairly rare that God actually works in this way (Brownie points for anyone who can find out where in the Bible it did happen!). What we've found is that God prefers adventure to predictable and safe. God seems to like to mould our characters and our identities by leading us step by step along the path he has called us to follow. That way, we have to keep his presence right in the middle of our plans, instead of running off on our own. Sometimes he lets us make our own mind up about things, sometimes he lets us go the wrong way so we learn something, sometimes he clearly directs us through prophecy and sometimes he puts skills and desires into us so we can follow them. Despite the fact that society tells us that *what* we do is all important we must remember that what God is really interested in is *who we are*. Who we are is made up of what God says about us in the Bible (what we learned about identity in Life lesson 2), what we're good at, what our character is like, what our personality is like, the decisions we make and lots of other stuff. This lesson should get you thinking about who God made you to be.

Write down or draw a picture of who you want to be (not a job or a career but the kind of person you want to be).

Now read the verse below.

God planned for them [YOU] to be like his Son;
and those he planned to be like his Son, he also
called; and those he called, he also made right with
him; and those he made right, he also glorified.
(Romans 8:30)

Rewrite that verse in your own words:

What do you think it means?

Gracefully received

To begin with, make a list of your gifts and talents. If you need some help, you could phone a friend, as the chances are they may spot them more readily than you. You may also want to refer to the lists of gifts in Romans 12:6–8 or 1 Corinthians 12.

Now rate each of these gifts/talents on a scale of 0 to 10, not based on the 'quality' of your giftings but on how much you are using them at this point in your life.

This exercise surprised me. There was so much of me that I was ignoring. Bring each of these areas to God in prayer, and together work on a strategy for increasing the use of your underused rusty giftings and talents. Like the old Fiesta that sits outside my house, the longer you leave something unused, the harder it is to restart.

Holding your giftings so close that they get mixed up in your own insecurities is a danger here, as opposed to holding them lightly as a gift. Holding gifts too close leads to a classic reaction when someone compliments you in regard to their use. Some folks will quickly reject the compliment stating that 'Actually, it wasn't that great', point out all the mistakes they made, or say something like 'it's not me, it's God'. **YOUR GIFTS HAVE BEEN GIVEN TO YOU BY GOD**, so I think he cries when we don't enjoy the fact that we have them. It would be like Santa Claus overhearing us in conversation with our friends on Boxing Day saying 'Nah, the bike isn't that great really – you see the brakes squeak a bit,' and 'I'm just not sure about the colour.' It is so easy to indulge in false humility, subconsciously seeking further affirmation. I have learned that often the simple right response in these situations is to say 'Thank you.'

Were there spiritual gifts in those biblical lists that you desire? Be honest and ask God for them.

Even though you are bad, you know how to give good gifts to your children. How much more will your heavenly Father give good gifts to those who ask him!
(Matthew 7:11)

Andy Flannagan, *God 360°*, Spring Harvest & Authentic, 2006

ReactionReactionReactionReaction

CIRCLE:

😊 😦 😐 😮 😕 😲

TICK:

Total rubbish ☐   Not sure ☐   Worth thinking about ☐   Genius ☐

FILL:

....

....

....

....

....

Name: **Charlie-Ann Waite**

Age: **14**

Town: **Sunderland**

Passions: **Animals, drama**

If you were a sandwich what kind of sandwich would you be?

BLT

Caramel digestives or chocolate Hobnobs?

Chocolate Hobnobs

What is the weirdest thing about boys?

They're obsessed with food.

What are you tempted by?

Chocolate.

When are you most tempted by chocolate?

When I'm on a diet.

When was the last time you were on a diet?

Yesterday.

Spirit reflections

Chip talks

A true man of God has several important qualities, but I'm only going to mention five of them now – integrity, humility, compassion, courage and zeal.

Integrity: a man of God is a man of his word. If he says he's going to do something, he does it – no matter what, even if it costs him. Take a minute to think about just how honest you really are. When you make a promise, do you keep it? Have you got your priorities right? A very wise man once told me that whenever I'm doing the right thing for God, he'll probably respond by giving me tons of new opportunities and saying, 'Choose one.' Then it's up to me to choose wisely.

Humility: a man of God is able to lead with a servant's heart – in other words, possessing the attitude and disposition of a servant. A servant is genuinely more concerned with making those around him feel as relaxed as possible, just like a true gentleman. When was the last time you knelt down to pray? Have you ever sat on the floor so that someone else could have a seat? It's important to recognise authority, and always be aware that you have to answer to somebody. If you haven't done so already, find someone who is willing to be your mentor, preferably older and wiser than you – and who's been a Christian for longer than you.

Compassion: a man of God has a heart for those less fortunate than himself. He cares when other people don't care. He prays for the lonely, poor and lost ones as if he was right there alongside them. Have you ever felt genuine concern for a homeless person? Do you ever give money to beggars? Many times, Jesus' biggest motivation for teaching big crowds (and even doing miracles for them) was sheer compassion. He was willing to sacrifice his own comfort for theirs.

Courage: a man of God stands up for what he believes is right. Wherever he sees injustice at work, he doesn't mind being the first one to do something about it. He isn't ashamed to do what others might shy away from. When in your life have you had the guts to defend someone who's being bullied? Did you do the honourable thing? Jim Yost, a missionary to Papua New Guinea, says that he wants his gravestone to read: 'Here lies Jim Yost. He never played it safe.' Be like that! Show some courageous love.

Passion: a man of God knows how to be passionate about something! One of the biggest misconceptions of Christianity is that it's boring and irrelevant. I wonder how much of this is due to the fact that there aren't enough young men rising up to be the warriors God intended for us to be? Get excited every once in a while! When was the last time you were accused of being over-enthusiastic about something? Extreme times call for extreme measures. But remember, enthusiasm without knowledge is not good (Proverbs 19:2).

Reaction Reaction Reaction Reaction

CIRCLE:

TICK:

Total rubbish ☐   Not sure ☐   Worth thinking about ☐   Genius ☐

FILL:

....

....

....

....

....

It's all about relationship

Jesus has an amazing relationship with God the Father. Time after time he proclaimed the richness and intensity of the relationship they shared. John 8:26,28,29 says 'I tell people only the things I have heard from the One who sent me, and he speaks the truth . . . know that these things I do are not by my own authority but that I say only what the Father has taught me. The One who sent me is with me. I always do what is pleasing to him, so he has not left me alone.' Luke tells us that Jesus often sought a lonely place to pray. The communion Jesus experienced with the Father was so intimate that he stated 'The Father and I are one' (John 10:30). At the cross, that relationship was ripped apart as Jesus actually became sin for us (2 Corinthians 5:21). Moments before he died, he cried to his Father, 'My God, why have you rejected me?' (Matthew 27:46). Communion with God had stopped and Jesus knew it immediately.

I'm not very good at remembering to charge my phone. It's not exactly unheard of for me to be chatting away and realise that I have been talking to a piece of plastic for the past few minutes without noticing that my battery has died. Feeling fairly embarrassed, I quickly stuff my phone in my pocket and hope that no one around me has realised that I have been talking to myself! Often I can go hours without even thinking about God, a whole day without fixing my attention solely on him. If the presence of God were to leave me, it would probably take me an age for it to dawn on me that he had gone.

We all have access to the most privileged relationship in the world, a relationship with our Creator. Yet we don't always take advantage of that fact. In the height of busyness, stress and fast-paced lifestyles, our prayer life is often the first thing to go. John Wesley understood the purpose of prayer. He would get up every day to pray for 2 hours from 5 a.m. till 7 a.m. If he had a busy day ahead, he wouldn't skip it, instead he would get up at four! We are told that when he was tired, Jesus would go and pray instead of going for a quick nap. That's where his strength and his compassion for people came from. God is waiting for you to let him be God in the situations you find yourself in. Chase after him in prayer and he promises that you will find him.

Andy Frost and Jo Wells, *Freestyle*, Authentic, 2005

CIRCLE:

TICK:

Total rubbish ☐   Not sure ☐   Worth thinking about ☐   Genius ☐

FILL:

....

....

....

....

....

IS THERE A WAY TO GOD'S WILL?

Bible Reading: Jeremiah 29:11–14

When you search for me with all your heart, you will find me!
(Jeremiah 29:13)

Jason just started his senior year of high school. Since he was eight, he was sure he wanted to study biology – until he actually took biology, that is, and found that he had to do dissections with one hand on the knife and the other holding his nose.

Besides that discouraging experience, Jason keeps hearing about the poor job outlook for biologists and the high educational requirements to succeed in the field. When his older sister lands a high paying computer job straight out of technical school Jason thinks about bypassing college altogether. And on top of everything else Jason wonders what God thinks of any of his plans for his life.

Jason faces some of the same choices you might face soon. And he's asking the biggest question about his future: Where does God want me to head in life?

'How can I know God's will?' is a question Christian leaders often hear from students. Some talk about it. Others worry about it. Some even lose sleep over it. These students burst with sincere, serious questions about God's will.

Why is God's will such a big deal for people your age? Because you face the three most important decisions of your life:

1. You're deciding who will guide your life – your Master. If you've trusted Jesus Christ as Saviour and Lord and intend to live your life according to his Word, you're headed in the right direction.

2. You're deciding if you will marry and whom you will marry – your mate. A marriage decision is doubly difficult because it takes two to tie the knot. You both have to see God's will the same way.

3. You're deciding what you will do with your life – your mission – and what preparation you need to accomplish your goals.

GOD LOVES YOU AND HAS A GREAT PLAN FOR YOUR LIFE. Jeremiah 29:11 declares, '"I know what I am planning for you," says the LORD. "I have good plans for you, not plans to hurt you. I will give you hope and a good future".' God also promised, 'I will make you wise and show you where to go. I will guide you and watch over you' (Psalm 32:8).

Even if you aren't yet wallowing in confusion about God's will, you can plan on facing some questions about how to spend your life. You can also plan that God will be with you to figure out the answers.

REFLECT: WHAT KIND OF PLANS DOES GOD HAVE FOR YOUR LIFE?

PRAY: HAVE YOU EVER TOLD GOD YOU WANT TO DO HIS WILL BEFORE YOU EVEN KNOW WHAT IT IS? NOW WOULD BE A GREAT TIME TO DO THAT.

Josh McDowell, *Youth Devotions 2*, Tyndale House, 2003

Reaction Reaction Reaction Reaction

CIRCLE:

😊 😞 😐 😮 😕 😲

TICK:

Total rubbish ☐ Not sure ☐ Worth thinking about ☐ Genius ☐

FILL:

....

....

....

....

Hidden pearls

'In our day, the pressure wasn't on to be like people on TV. I would say really if you are a keen Christian, think to yourself, do you really want to be like that person on the TV? What's he like? Is he a Christian, is Jesus at the centre of his life? If the answer is no, you would be better off identifying yourself with Jesus and not with someone who's popular on the screen.'

DON'T FOLLOW THE CROWD

Helen talks

What you do in life and the decisions you make will have a massive impact on *who* you become as a person. Now I don't mean if you decide to become an astronaut you will suddenly develop a different personality than if you had become a teacher, but the choices you make about how you spend your time will impact which talents you will develop and how your character develops.

When I say character I mean the stuff that comes out when you are squeezed! For example, when you are under pressure do you blame everyone else, or have you built responsibility and perseverance into your character? When you feel hurt are you like a wounded animal lashing out at everyone around you, or have you built patience and forgiveness into your character? Character traits are the things we learn (or choose not to learn), things God's Spirit will develop in us like love, joy, peace, patience, kindness, goodness, faithfulness, gentleness, self control (Galatians 5:22,23, look it up).

When I was 18, I accepted a place at Leeds University to study environmental management. Like most people, I'd grown up in school with the idea that you really should go straight to university or college after school and then you should get a good sensible job that could pay the bills. I decided to take one year out before uni to go to America to a Bible college and performing arts school to continue studying mime and dance. Anyway, one year turned into two, which turned into marrying Chip, which turned into working for Innervation Trust and thebandwithnoname and in the end I never got to Leeds University. However, because of my experience of working, touring and performing, I managed to get on to a Masters degree course (a second degree that you usually can only do after doing a 3-year Bachelor's degree) in Arts Management by flexible learning. I managed to finish the degree and get a good grade whilst working 4 days a week doing ministry!

I am so not saying this to brag and tell you all how clever I am, far from it. What I want to point out is that I am a totally different person now than I would have turned out to be had I taken the route that everyone expected me to take (school, uni/college, job). I have travelled the world, I get to dance for my job, I have learned to trust God for my finances, I've learned patience by teaching people, I've learned perseverance by helping to build Innervation from two staff to thirty, I learned discipline from having to study at home and I've learned to work in a team in difficult circumstances. I'm not sure I would have developed all those character traits if I had taken the usual route through life. I think I would have got some of them but definitely not all.

Please don't think (especially the parents reading this) that I'm saying university is a waste of time or that you shouldn't get a good job. I'm not. I'm just saying that you have to decide what is right for you rather than being carried along by what everyone else is doing. **I WOULD DEFINITELY RECOMMEND TAKING A YEAR OR TWO YEARS OUT BEFORE GOING TO UNIVERSITY.** Not taking time out just to doss around, but having a year where you dedicate yourself to God, putting yourself in completely new situations and getting out of your comfort zone will help you develop good character traits. It will help you learn about the world, get a different perspective and find out more about who you are and who you want to become. When you do finally go to university, college or employment you will be there because you know it's what you're called to do and you will have the maturity to do it well rather than just doing it because you were told to.

There are absolutely loads of organisations that are desperate for volunteers. For us at Innervation, recruiting staff is the one thing that holds us up from doing more evangelism more than anything else. Think about what your gifts are and dedicate them to God for a year. Here are some example organisations you could look into (but there are tons more).

ORGANISATION	WHO THEY NEED	WHAT YOU DO
Innervation Trust www.innervation.org	Singers, dancers, MCs, musicians, sound engineers, team leaders	Work in schools for 2 years doing evangelism
Eden Project (the Message) www.message.org.uk	Anyone with a heart for evangelism	Live alongside the most deprived people as an Eden youth worker
Youth For Christ www.yfc.co.uk	Performers, sports people, youth workers, children's workers	Sports teams, bands, drama teams, overseas missions, youth work, prisons work, you name it
YWAM www.ywam-england.com	Anyone	Mission and discipleship training
Oasis Trust www.oasistrust.org	Anyone	UK and international mission and community work with street kids, the homeless, the poor

Reaction Reaction Reaction Reaction

CIRCLE:

TICK:

Total rubbish ☐   Not sure ☐   Worth thinking about ☐   Genius ☐

FILL:

....

....

....

....

Your story

Read chapters 2 – 4 of the book of Jonah.

Have you ever wondered who wrote the book of Jonah? Was his secretary stuck in the whale with him? Unless he had a camera crew following him around, there really are only two ways that we could know everything that we do about him in such detail. Either he wrote it himself in the third person (and with his mood swings, I wouldn't be surprised), or he took the time to describe accurately to a scribe what happened to him.

Have you ever written down your story? The story of how God has taken you from where you were to where you are? We seem to constantly live 'in the moment' these days, and what is most important to us is only what is current. However, we have so much to learn from looking back and appreciating our own journey. What changes have you seen, what blessings have you received? What has been joyful and what has been painful? When did growth happen? Who were the key players? What were the shipwrecks, and what were the moments of bravery? Just because there are no **MASSIVE MAMMALIAN ENCOUNTERS**, your story is no less important.

Spend a decent bit of time doing this. As a target, aim for 500 words, but if it ends up much longer, then no problem. Look to see if there are common themes running through experiences and relationships that perhaps you've never seen before. Once you've done it, share it with someone. You may be surprised how much it will encourage you and others. It may also make you more confident in sharing your story on an ad hoc basis in conversation. However, more than anything else today, simply share your story with God. Rejoice in how he has been faithful. Bring him the highs and the lows, and thank him that at the end of the day, he is the ultimate Author.

Andy Flannagan, *God 360°*, Spring Harvest & Authentic, 2006

Reaction Reaction Reaction Reaction

CIRCLE:

TICK:

Total rubbish ☐   Not sure ☐   Worth thinking about ☐   Genius ☐

FILL:

....

....

....

....

....

Reality Check

WHEN I GROW UP, I WANNA BE . . .

This reality check should help you get an idea about who you want to become.

List five things you'd like to be when you grow up, in order of preference. (Here's a clue – what are you passionate about? What's the first thing you think about when you wake up? Breakfast doesn't count!)

1. . . . .

2. . . . .

3. . . . .

4. . . . .

5. . . . .

Now circle five character traits you think will be important in your top three choices.

Patience	Hard work	Honesty	Tact	Generosity
Kindness	Serving	Humility	Organisation	Leadership
Courageous	Humour	Resourceful	Stubborn	Loyal
Caring	Unselfish	Confident	Respectful	Considerate
Imaginative	Inventive	Creative	Independent	Honest
Friendly	Adventurous	Responsible	Helpful	Neat
Cooperative	Ambitious	Curious	Determined	Energetic
Thoughtful	Cheerful	Childlike	Clarity	Reliable
Team player	Outgoing	Calm	Introverted	Witty

Without showing what you've circled, ask an honest relative or close friend to tell you what they think your five best character traits are. Write down what they say.

1..

2..

3..

4..

5..

How does their list compare to yours?

What practical steps can you take to develop the character traits you need. (For example, to develop generosity give away something you really like.)

....

....

....

....

....

Remember, God is more interested in who you are than what you do. Ask him to help you develop a character that reflects and honours him.

What if?

'I say this because I know what I am planning for you,' says the LORD. 'I have good plans for you, not plans to hurt you. I will give you hope and a good future.'

(Jeremiah 29:11)

4

First up

We all know that sometimes we mess up, we go wrong and we don't follow God's plan. Maybe it's just us, but after you've really gone wrong, don't you start to wonder if all those great things God says about you are still true, or if all those plans he had were dependent on us going the right way? Does it all become null and void if we don't manage to follow God and do the right thing? Read the verse below:

> Brothers and sisters, look at what you were when God called you. Not many of you were wise in the way the world judges wisdom. Not many of you had great influence. Not many of you came from important families.
>
> (1 Corinthians 1:26)

Does God expect us to be perfect before he can use us? (circle one)

Yes   No   Not sure

> God never changes his mind about the people he calls and the things he gives them. At one time you refused to obey God. But now you have received mercy, because those people refused to obey.
>
> (Romans 11:29,30)

What an amazing verse! What a merciful and forgiving God we have.

Write Romans 11:29,30 out in your own words and include your name in the translation (for example, put your name instead of the word 'people'):

Name: **Alice Chant**

Age: **16**

Town: **Devon**

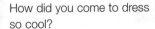

How did you come to dress so cool?

I was influenced by my grandmother.

What do you like to do in your spare time?

I sit and talk to a poster on the wall at school (which is my room). I'm home-schooled.

How do you hear the voice of God?

With two cans on the end of a string. Not really. I lie in bed and look up at the sky.

What was the last thing God said to you?

This morning, he said to me to go and tell one of the youth group to go and jump in the swimming pool of God. And not just be dipping his toes in.

What does that mean?

Hurry up and become a Christian!

PEOPLE CLIP

Bible reading: Isaiah 43:1–4

Don't be afraid, because I have saved you.
I have called you by name and you are mine.
(Isaiah 43:1)

University of California football player Roy Riegles made Rose Bowl history back in 1929. In the second quarter of the game, he scooped up a Georgia Tech fumble and headed for the end zone – the *wrong* end zone. He was tackled – by a team mate – just before crossing the goal line. Riegels's mistake would have earned Georgia Tech 6 points. Riegels's team had to punt from their own end zone. Georgia Tech blocked the kick, resulting in a two-point safety – points that eventually won the game for Georgia Tech.

D uring halftime, the California players filed glumly into the dressing room, Reigels slumped in a corner, buried his face in his hands, and sobbed uncontrollably. Coach Price offered no halftime pep talk. What could he say? As the team got ready to go out for the second half, his only comment was, 'Men, the same team that played the first half will start the second.'

The players started for the door, all but Roy Riegels. Coach Price walked to the corner where Riegels sat and said quietly, 'Roy, didn't you hear me?'

'COACH, I CAN'T DO IT,' Roy said dejectedly. 'I have ruined you, the university, and myself. I can't face that crowd again to save my life.'

Coach Price put his hand on the player's shoulder. 'Roy, get up and go back; the game is only half over.' Inspired by his coach's confidence, Roy Riegels went out to play again. After the game, the Georgia Tech players commented that Riegels played harder in the second half than they had ever seen anyone play.

What you see in Coach Price is just a glimmer of God's accepting attitude towards us. We make mistakes. Once in a while we run the wrong way. And when we stumble and fall, we make the problem worse by shrinking from God in shame. But he comes to us and says, 'Get up and keep going; the game is only half over.' That's unconditional love. And as you receive and enjoy God's unconditional love, you see more clearly that you are unconditionally lovable!

In Isaiah 43:1, God commits to love and accept you. He says to you, 'I have called you by name, and you are mine.' You can personalise the verse this way: 'The God of the universe has called me by name, he says I belong to him.'

God doesn't disown you when you go the wrong way. He never says, 'You blew it, so you don't belong to me any longer.' Sure, he wants you to turn around and go the right way, but he puts his Spirit inside you to get you going again. But he never says anything but, 'You belong to me; you are mine.'

REFLECT: THINK OF AN AREA WHERE YOU'VE BLOWN IT. WHAT DOES GOD THINK OF YOUR NOT BEING PERFECT?

PRAY: THANK GOD THAT HE STILL BELIEVES IN YOU EVEN WHEN YOU BLOW IT.

Josh McDowell, *Youth Devotions 2*, Tyndale House, 2003

Reaction Reaction Reaction Reaction

CIRCLE:

TICK:

Total rubbish ☐   Not sure ☐   Worth thinking about ☐   Genius ☐

FILL:

....

....

....

....

....

On the outside looking in

Bible reading: Mark 6:1–6

(Mark 6:4)

Logan and his classmate Olivia were chubby, brainy and homely. When year-book time rolled around, the two students were voted the most perfectly matched pair in their middle school, even thought they hardly knew each other.

So when Logan and Olivia showed up hand in hand at the last dance of the school year, the kids snickered. And when the couple stepped into the dance area and awkwardly tried to move their uncoordinated bodies to the music, the crowd exploded. Finally, Olivia grabbed her partner by the hand and snorted, 'Come on, Logan!' The laughter should have ended there. Except Logan tripped and dragged Olivia to the ground with him. And they both bounced.

U nless you count yourself among the world's cruel elite, you probably wince when you see a pair like Logan and Olivia mocked. You might not have this pair's problems, but surely you know what it means to feel unwanted and unloved.

It's hard to believe that Jesus could have faced that kind of rejection. But the apostle John says it bluntly: 'HE CAME TO THE WORLD THAT WAS HIS OWN, BUT HIS OWN PEOPLE DID NOT ACCEPT HIM' (John 1:11). The residents of planet Earth have erected a kind of 'You don't belong here' sign to their Creator, and if you check out Mark 6, you see that Jesus was even rejected by the people of Nazareth, the town where he grew up.

When you're a Christian, you have to get ready for some rejection. Jesus didn't leave any doubts that at times the world would snub – even hate – his followers: 'I have chosen you out of the world, so you don't belong to it. That is why the world hates you' (John 15:19). When a friend finds out that you won't cut class with him because you figure obeying Christ means showing up for school, he might cut you off his list of friends. When a group of girlfriends discovers you don't have any personal sexual adventures to brag about, they might kick you out in the cold. Your loyalty, purity, honesty, and dependability as a Christian will make you look as laughable to some people as Logan and Olivia looked to their peers.

There's better news though. Jesus promised a special blessing and rewards for his rejected followers (see Matthew 5:11,12). You can coast along as a camouflaged Christian, dodging confrontation and rejection. But if you take a stand for what's right – even if it means losing popularity, friends, or status – you're in line for eternally significant rewards.

REFLECT: AS A CHRISTIAN YOU ARE GUARANTEED TO FACE REJECTION. WHAT MAKES IT WORTH IT?

PRAY: ASK GOD TO MAKE YOU STRONG EVEN IN THE FACE OF REJECTION FOR YOUR FAITH.

Josh McDowell, *Youth Devotions 2*, **Tyndale House, 2003**

ReactionReactionReactionReaction

CIRCLE:

TICK:

Total rubbish ☐   Not sure ☐   Worth thinking about ☐   Genius ☐

FILL:

....
....
....
....
....

Last up

At the start of this book we said we were going to look at some of the basic needs of acceptance and identity. Hopefully by now, having read all the extracts and filled in all the reaction boxes, you have a good idea about what God says about you and your identity. You know that he made you, that you are unique and that he has a special plan just for you. We hope that now you aren't focusing on how to get people to accept you, but that you believe what God says about you, which is so much more important than what people think. Make sure you get yourself around people who are going to help you as you try to base your identity in God, rather than people who will pull you away from him, or put you down. Get some positive role models in your life and continue on in the adventure of finding out who God made you to be.

Pray

Lord God, thank you that you made me exactly the way you want me to be. Thank you that you have planned something great for me in my life and I am the only one who can walk the path you have designed for me. Please help me to keep my identity based in you. Give me good role models who I can aspire to be like, help me not to compare myself to others and continue to make me grow to be more like you. Amen.